LONG
WAY
HOME

Also by Pat Schneider

LIBRETTI

The Lament of Michal
Autumn Setting

PLAYS

A Question of Place
Berries Red
Dream: The Musical

POETRY

White River Junction

NON-FICTION

In Our Own Voices: Writings of Women in Housing Projects
A Writer Is Someone Who Writes: Writing Alone and With Others

LONG WAY HOME

Poems by

Pat Schneider

Amherst Writers & Artists Press

Amherst, Massachusetts

Copyright 1993 by Pat Schneider
ALL RIGHTS RESERVED
Amherst Writers & Artists Press
P.O. Box 1076
Amherst, Massachusetts 01004
ISBN 0-941895-11-4
FIRST EDITION
Designed by Barbara Werden
Printed and bound by Hamilton I. Newell Printing

The publication of this book was made possible in part by a grant from the Massachusetts Cultural Council as administered by the Amherst Arts Council.

Some of these poems have appeared in the following publications, to whose editors grateful acknowledgement is made for permission to reprint: "About, Among Other Things, God," in *Colorado State Review*; "River" in *Weather Report (Anthology)*; "Richard" in *Slant*; "Sound of the Night Train" in *Negative Capability* ; "Fire" in *Up Against the Wall, Mother*; "Gravity" in *XANADU, (Anthology)*; "Imagine a Hallway in Childhood" in *Poets On . . .* ; "Boy" in *Embers* and *Peregrine*; "Truth Enough" in *Devil's Millhopper*; "Overnight" in *Cotton Boll/Atlanta Review*; "Tomita: Pictures" in *Slant*; "Grasses Like a Curtain" in *The MacGuffin*; "First Born" (as "Silent Retreat") in *Sing, Heavenly Muse*; "Going Home the Longest Way Around" in *Nomad* and *Storytelling Journal*; "Trouble" in *Peregrine*; "This Flight" and "There is Another Way" in *Kalliope*; "The Trail" in *Fractals*; "Things the Wind Does" in *Women of the Fourteenth Moon (Anthology)*, "Lucia Theresa" in *Life on the Line* (Anthology) "Máire, Who Feeds the Wild Cat" in *If I Had My Life to Live Over, I Would Pick Daisies*. The following poems were published in a chapbook titled *White River Junction* by Amherst Writers & Artists Press: "Sweet Potato Pie;" "Sarah Laughed;" "The Face of the Other;" "Braided Rug," and "Death as Houseplant."

For Peter

CONTENTS

About, Among Other Things, God   1

RIVER

River   5
Richard   6
Emma   8
The Aunts   9
Lelah at Eighteen: 1922   11
Cyclone   12
Sound of the Night Train   13
In My Father's House   15
"The Things We Do . . ."   16
Fire   18
Poem for Mother on the Forty Ninth Day   19
The Grandmother   20

GRAVITY

Gravity   23
Imagine a Hallway in Childhood   25
Miss Low   27
Tomorrow, Just You Wait . . .   29
Chinese Lantern   32

FROM THE OUTSIDE NOW

From the Outside Now   35
Sweet Potato Pie   36
Boy   37
Henderson Settlement   39
Saturday Night   41
I Am Missing You   43
At the Sea of Galilee: 1976   44
Máire, Who Feeds the Wild Cat   45

Sarah Laughed 46
Letting Go 48
Personal Address 49
Dear Lover, Dear God 50

TRUTH ENOUGH

Truth Enough 53
Ornament 55
Pond in the River 56
Letter to a Son in College 57
Shape and Line. Tomorrow 58
Overnight 60
Tomita: Pictures 61
To a High School Senior 62
Grasses Like a Curtain 63
After All, the Leaves 65
Child 66
First Born 67

THE FACE OF THE OTHER

The Face of the Other 71
Going Home the Longest Way Around 73
White River Junction 74
A Blessing 77
Braided Rug 78
Trouble 80
Lucia Theresa 81
Wild Wolves Howling 82
Don't Look at the Moon 83
Death as Houseplant 84
Bridge 86

THIS FLIGHT

This Flight 89
Welcoming Angels 90
The Trail 91
Things the Wind Does 92
First Cousin 93
Midsummer 94
There is Another Way 96

ABOUT, AMONG OTHER THINGS, GOD

Come.
The primrose blooms in the garden.
The mourning dove calls in the sycamore tree.

Rain on the sill of the window,
Sounds of every kind of weather
are sweet in this old house.
Come.

In the pantry, jars of beans,
lentils, sunflower seeds. Sesame. Jars
of preserves, small cans
of spices stand in rows.

It is here.

A woman stands in the doorway
and calls. Her apron bleached from washings
and from hanging in the sun. Behind her,
through the doorway, the house
is dark and cool, and the word
that she calls into the late afternoon,
into the shadows gathering under the lilacs,
into the long, long shadow of the sycamore tree
is come.
Come home.

RIVER

RIVER

A delicate fuzz of fog
like mold, or moss,
all across the river
in this early light.
Another day, I might
have still been sleeping.

What a pity. How the stars
and seas and rivers
in their fragile lace of fog
go on without us
morning after morning,
year after year.
And we disappear.

RICHARD

Grandpa had a big mouth.
When he opened up his country store
in the middle of the night
and handed patent medicine to Amos Washington
after Doc Davis called out through his back screen door
I don't doctor niggers,
somebody put a bundle of sticks
on Grandpa's porch.

And there was nobody in southern Oklahoma
in 1908 didn't know that was the warning of the KKK.

But that didn't alter Grandpa.
Not a bit.

Mama says he used to walk the floor all night
trying to figure out who married Cain
and why a God of love
would drown the greater part of His creation
and how Methuselah could have lived
past eight hundred ninety-nine.

Until he gave it up
for Darwin and the Socialists
and dragged Grandma down to Louisiana
to a colony where there was no private property
and it was one for all and all for one,
except Grandma saw the Socialist Director
in full moonlight steal his own muskmelons.
Milk was rationed, and everybody shared,
but Grandpa died down there, of something

that they called The Sugar Diabetes.
Afterwards, Mama asked Grandma
if she should go to heaven and could have
either of her husbands — grandpa, or
the first one, who died when they were young —
which one would she choose?

Mama could remember
how Grandpa knocked Grandma down the stairs
one time, then cried about it after,
and lost the farm that her first husband left
and nearly drove her crazy
with his everlasting being in the right
about the niggers and the Bible
and the evils of baptism
the Origin of the Species
and Eugene V. Debs.

Oh, I'd take Richard, Grandma said.
I lived with him so long.
But she had to think a while
before she spoke.

EMMA

Emma Ridgway saved tin foil
from every stick of gum.
She wrapped it on a ball of foil
she was making, to help the country
win the Second World War.

She got quieter as she got old.
She never told me anything,
but I heard stories:
how her father cut the ruffles off her dresses
so the folks he preached to wouldn't think
his daughter put on airs;
how her husband knocked her down the stairs
when she disagreed with him
and took her to a colony
to live where milk was rationed
a half pint every day if you were old,
a pint if you were pregnant.

Emma Ridgway divided every stick of gum
in halves. She said
all a person needed was a little at a time.
When she died, she left
two small dresser drawers half full
of all of her belongings
and a coat that was too big for her
and one extra pair of shoes.

THE AUNTS

The aunts stand in a half circle
just behind her chair.
Their memories are in their faces, how
they do not love each other.
The camera doesn't catch the filling station
with its back room where she is going to die,
but it's right there, off the snapshot
to her left. Her grandson,
fresh from bombing missions over Germany
jumped out the upstairs window
the night the station burned. The aunts
were sorry all her handmade quilts were gone.
They built the station back up right away
and added room for grocery shelves,
cans of sardines, Sunshine bread and
an ice chest full of soda pop, up front.
Had to. It was business. It was
1947, Fort Leonard Wood the next mile
down on Highway sixty-six, soldiers
and their women renting little trailer
houses all around the place. You can't see
them, either, in the photograph.
It is a close up. Just her face,
lower than the others, and older. She is
seated, but you can't see her chair.
And all around her, the faces of the aunts,
smiling. They were children before Henry Ford
thought up his Model T. They rode the wagon
into town, legs hanging off the back,
long stockings on their arms to keep

their skin all white. They dreamed
of being ladies. In the photograph they are
middle aged, plump around the waist, together
for the last time. It doesn't matter.
They do not love each other. Even so,
when they lean in close like that,
you almost could imagine
they make a kind of crown around her head.

LELAH AT EIGHTEEN: 1922

In this one you are young.
You stand on a tree stump
laughing. There is sun
light on your hair. In this one
you have not been saved
at a Baptist tent revival.
You are not religious. You
have not cut off the beads
from your favorite party dress
nor pulled your long hair back
into a bun. In this one
you have not decided that you are
too tall, too bold, too worldly.

You have not yet decided that
the boy who stands beside you
is a sinner. You have not yet
given back his ring. He is the boy
you will dream about
after you are eighty.

CYCLONE

The night the cyclone ripped
around the house, big oaks
and sycamores went down
on all four sides. I remember
Mama happy, then, for days.
Almost as if that's what she'd like to do —
tear up a lot of trees without hurting anyone,
and then, before the daylight came,
simply disappear.

In another lifetime, or in the one
she had, but in another sex,
she would have been inventor,
discoverer, anything but Mama.

She made hominy out in the yard:
black belly of the cast iron pot,
hot coals, her attentive hover.
She made lye soap out there, too,
drew water up ninety-seven feet and
gave it to the goat, because the goat
was more particular than the cow,
and wouldn't drink at all
if there was jersey drool
in the watering trough.

Mama made hominy once.
She made lye soap once.
She canned corn on the cob, once, too,
just to see if she could do it.

Nothing that turned out good
was ever done again.

SOUND OF THE NIGHT TRAIN

Only once in every twenty four hours the train comes through my town — in the dark, still, center of the night. Sometimes I am awake to hear it, it's wail a long sound-tunnel back to another time, another place.

1934. Early March in southern Missouri, northern Arkansas. The air cold, the night wind hard in the open doorway of a boxcar headed south toward Louisiana.

My mother told me this in the winter of her dying. Always she had said my father was *just no good* — her Ozark accent persisting to the end: a woman *warshed and rinched* the clothes. A man who didn't treat a woman right was *just no good*.

It was the heart of the Depression, she said. *I never did tell this to anyone — I was so ashamed. We wanted to go to see Papa and Mama in the Socialist Colony down in Louisiana, but we didn't have any money. So we rode the rails. One night a man in the boxcar with us said, "If you-all know what's good for you, you'll jump right now." We were scared; we jumped. And me six months pregnant with you. Isn't that awful?*

She lay very still, then, on her high hospital bed, the wedding ring quilt she had pieced when her eyes were good pulled up around her shoulders. What made me sad, listening to this story, was the strangeness of my mother's not saying, *He was just no good.* For the first time in her eighty-six years she said, *He was good to me then. I was cold, and we were sleeping on the ground. He covered me with leaves.*

She died soon after she told me that story. I listen now sometimes for the sound of the night train, as if that long moan were a tunnel back to that young woman, that young man, in the middle of the five short years that they were married, and he was good to her, he covered her — covered me — with leaves.

IN MY FATHER'S HOUSE

In my father's house, the worms
go in and out, in and out,
the cleaning women of the underworld.
They are cleaning the rooms of my father.
The clean bones will be rafters
and the sky will give its sunlight and its rain
to the chambers where the heart no longer lives.
My father's heart, my heart
is no longer native to his skeleton.
Where the quick life of the chipmunk, the field mouse,
the owl, where those lives have gone
he, too, has gone
and I have given notice to my body
of an impending change of permanent address.

I will follow my father.

In his life, he gave me
his absence. In his death,
he is helpless; I will plunder his grave,
claim him as mine. I am his firstborn.
I say to the children of his second marriage,
Stand back! It's my turn for a father.
I will write him into a poem,
I will make believe that he loved me.
Now that he is mine, I will celebrate
the rafters of his ribs, the bare room
of his brain, the long, still question mark
of spine, the finger bones, the quiet
in the narrow room of his
abandoned sex.

"THE THINGS WE DO..."

My mother stumbles through the rain,
her hand on her cane, shoulders
hunched beneath her short white coat,
her left eye blind now from glaucoma.

Donatello carved a Mary Magdalene
no one had imagined: old, tired,
not at all a virgin or a saint. And
made his Jesus like a working man.
Bruneschelli chided: *You put a peasant
on the cross, not the Saviour.*
Donatello, overcome, dropped the eggs
he had been carrying, and tried to do things right.

This morning my mother cried on the telephone,
*I had an involuntary bowel movement, and
I didn't even know it.* Her short white coat,
her bare hand on the rain-soaked metal rail,
the way she holds herself walking up the steps
to the eye doctor's office.

She is singing as we come out. The doctor
teased her, and they laughed together.
Her bare hand slides along the wet rail,
her head receives the rain.
Her steps are slow, slow, leaning on me,
leaning on the rail. She sings,
*It's raining, it's pouring,
the things we do are boring.*

Now it's night and the sound of the wind
is wonderful. The rain is in it.

Winter coming down from Canada
and all of January yet to come.

I am tired of perplexities.
I want the Mary and the Jesus
who are peasants, who are old.
I want the eggs to fly back up
into Donatello's apron.
I want Mary to sit down with me
and have a cup of tea.

A cup of tea, yes.
It's raining, it's pouring. Yes.
The world is too much with us, Wordsworth said,
and TV hadn't even been invented.

FIRE

Rain moves over the garden
I have neglected all summer long.

My brother's house burned to the ground
on Thursday. This rain
falls into the collapsed inversion
of his daily life.

My mother gives me morning reports
on life at Cozy Corner: who ate
the peeling as well as the banana,
who yelled for George all night long,
who cried, speechless, in the gerry-chair,
who died.

This rain wets the pansies someone planted
all the way around the nursing home.

My mother says, *Don't tell me
any more bad news.*
I say, There isn't any bad news, Mama.
She doesn't believe me. *Did my encyclopedia burn up in
the fire?* I say, Yes, it did.
Don't tell me any more bad news, she says.

Indiscriminate, this rain. In the garden,
a tangle of weeds. Young trees
I cannot bear to execute. For all they know,
they are the forefront of a forest.

Who am I to tell them it's not so?

POEM FOR MOTHER ON THE 49TH DAY

In folk wisdom, if the dead
are going to communicate,
it will happen on the forty-ninth day.
Today. I listen when the closet door
stands open, when the wind
moves new seed-pods on the maple tree,
when something in me moves,
I listen. But there is nothing.
No word of pardon or reprieve,
no curse, no blessing. No taking leave.

Your death is a hole in the universe
that all my rage runs through.
Now it sparkles in the black night
of my remembering, like stars,
as if something has been broken
and is spangled everywhere —
something that was hot, gone cold.
Old rage can be like that,
can light the night behind us
like dead stars gone out
whose light still reaches us
because we are so distant. Perhaps,
if I take a reading on them,
I will not lose my way.

THE GRANDMOTHER

*In response to a painting
by Gregory Gillespie*

Stripped down against that dark
To dark, she speaks.
Wearing a wild electric prophecy of hair
Untouched by hairdressers,
She speaks. Prophecy

Is the open end of past, and she is
Listening. What she hears
Was uttered on the other side of walls,
Outside slats of white venetian blinds,
Beyond the rungs of straight-backed kitchen chairs.

Her dress is brown. The neckline
Might have been an opening in earth,
Her neck might have been a sunflower stalk.
Her face is heavy with its weight of seeds,
Seasoned, balanced, remembering the sun.

She hears a voice that may have long ago gone out
The way a star goes dark and still we see its light.
Prophecy is listening and speaking as a single act,
Gathering in a light, a music that you never made,
And letting it go on.

GRAVITY

GRAVITY

> *Falling into gravity*
> *allows us to know weight.*
> —Beth Goren

> *A dream uninterpreted*
> *is a letter unopened.*
> —Talmud

I am a small man without a head
standing in the rain. I laugh
at the woman in the doorway
who worries that I will get rain
in my face. She doesn't understand.

I am a young woman walking
with a man who has no head.
He is pleasant enough,
but it is raining. I take
the cuff of his collar in my hand
and pull him away. I want to go.
I do not want to stand in the rain
any longer under the eyes
of the woman in the doorway
who will not shut her mouth.

I am a woman in a doorway.
There is a little man outside.
He has no head. His neck
is open, and hollow. It receives
rain. The woman beside him
is young. She grabs him
by his collar and pulls him along,

but she is not angry.
Nor does she seem unkind.
They both laugh at me when I say
to her, you are letting rain
fall on his face. I guess
it was a stupid thing to say,
but how do you say rain
is getting into his chest cavity?
They are leaving. I should have
asked them in, out of the weather.
I'm sorry they are going,
but I'm glad when they are gone.

I am a dreamer dreaming
myself standing in a doorway,
dreaming a dwarf with no head,
a young woman taking him away.

I am a woman remembering
a dream, trying to read
the letter. It is no use.
The language is foreign.
It comes from the place
where one falls into gravity
and knows weight.

IMAGINE A HALLWAY IN CHILDHOOD . . .

It is always the same goddamned hallway,
the same smell of darkness
at the center of my mind.

I won't go back there this time.
Not again.

I will make myself a hallway. Let it be
light. Let there be sun
falling through a window and carpeting
a stair. Let there be space and a clock
ticking fifteen minutes before noon.
Let it be morning. Let it be June.

Let there be biscuits baking in the kitchen
and the smell of nutmeg rampant in the house.
Let there be some dust between the rungs
at the stairway edge,
but only half a week's worth. No more.
Let there be a baby's picture book
abandoned on a table in the downstairs hall
and a slight puddle standing
at the tip of an umbrella
in an old umbrella stand.

Let there be privacy possible here,
let there be no Mr. Costello smelling
of cheap wine, grouchy, waiting in line
outside the bathroom door with his urine
in a milk bottle in his hand
let there be no stale smell of sauerkraut

from the room of the unhappy woman upstairs,
no screaming *Nigger! Nigger!*
coming up the furnace ducts
from the apartment below. Let there be
an absolute absence of cockroaches.
Let there be no fear of the police,
no chain lock on the door,
no grease across the windowpane.
Let there be no shame.

And it is so.

I have made a hallway for myself,
and I am walking down it.
I walk in sunlight and nutmeg. I walk
in the still magic of imagined space,
and almost at the end, on the left,
there is a door. It is standing open,
and I go in
and close the door behind me,

like this . . .

MISS LOW

Miss Low moved across the room
in front of our straight rows
of scarred oak desks and wooden seats
like General MacArthur reviewing his troops.

Her huge bosom refused to stay
beneath the edges of her cardigan.
She jerked the buttons toward the buttonholes
again and again as if her breasts
were recalcitrant students and the sweater
was her code of law, knit and purled
on long thin needles of her will.

We were seated by rank. Row one seat one
was always Jerry Stepman. He played violin,
wore glasses, spoke softly and seldom.
Row seven seat six was Andy Naegle or Eugene
Busch. They were always at the rear,
seemed to care the least, and clearly
would have talked together if they could,
if Miss Low had not walked so evenly
back and forth, back and forth,
jerking her bosom in.

Most of us ebbed and flowed within a range
of several seats. Once I made it to first row,
but that was just for three days, at the back.
Every act was judged. Any error, of
content or discretion, changed our seats.
The wrong expression on a person's face

could cause half the room to move.
If anyone moved up, everyone below moved down.
We tried to be invisible.

I learned a lot about the world that year.
The war was over. In a big room
at the *St. Louis Post-Dispatch*
I saw some awful pictures
of concentration camps. Later, I sat
and watched Miss Low's white hands
and for the first time had an inkling
of what was really going on.

TOMORROW, JUST YOU WAIT

Paint is peeling from the Victory marquee.
I drink a cup of coffee, waiting for a friend.
Cars pass, they are reflected
motion pictures in broken glass
across the street. Old cars
in this old town. South Holyoke.
The smell of two eggs over easy.

Plywood panels cover half the holes
in the movie house facade. Shreds
of some lost banner flap in a February wind.
Burned out neon tubing. Letters vaguely
red, white and blue on the marquee are still
announcing VICTORY and I am thinking
of old wars, and of my friend,
tying up the ends of marriage and divorce.

There must have been bright posters
in these windows when we were girls.
Lights and flags. Humphrey Bogart
in his prime. A man behind me laughs:

> *Forty years ago, . . .*

he says. He is eating eggs.

> *. . .the goddamned grease in*
> *the barracks kitchen . . .*
> *I almost threw up . . .*

He is remembering his war.

> *When we landed in England*
> *they put us in tents . . .*

The waitress, joking with him, sings

> *"There'll be bluebirds over*
> *The white cliffs of Dover,*
> *Tomorrow, just you wait and see."*

I sit remembering posters in the window
at the Booneville picture show. Distorted
faces: "Japs," and "Flying Tigers,"
large teeth painted on small airplanes
grinning at some grownup joke
I couldn't understand.

> *"Here we go, over the wild, blue yonder,*
> *At 'em, boys, give 'er the gun!"*

My father and my mother were at war
with one another; my generation
was born bloody in the heart
of battle.

The actor's name inside the weathered window box
could be Ronald Reagan. The jukebox
music in this dim cafe is out of date;
coffee, cheap and served with cream
is "regular." My friend slides sideways
back into the booth, says she has paid
Internal Revenue. We are veterans
of our generation's wars,
we are bruised, marked, go on
singing old songs.
We will not tear down the old Marquee;
the old cowboys, the old heros. It is we
who make them presidents and kings;

we were born to war, we will forever wave
the old flags, cry
Over easy, baby, over easy,
let's have a little homefries on the side,
tell the old tales, sing the old songs,
and yell across our coffee cups,
Just give us the usual

PHYSALIS ALKEKENGI: CHINESE LANTERN

for Margaret Robison

In this fragile, paper thin husk,
the color of autumn has lasted all winter.
Ice storm and snow and windchill breaking
the backs of maple, the great gray arms of pine,
this color has lasted. There is a place
between two ribs where the skeleton shows;
the stem is crooked, the seeds have all escaped,
but the color has lasted.

Today, driving down from the hills, Shelburne Falls,
Greenfield, Deerfield, Sunderland, you and I
sing old songs until laughter breaks to tears,
our voices cracking, our memory thin as paper.
We have lost the words, the lovely old silly clichés:
In a marketplace in old Algiers . . . , you cry,
howling with laughter, your voice too low
for me to reach, and neither of us can remember
what it was that rhymed with *old Algiers*
until halfway through September Song
I yell, *photographs and souvenirs* and Margaret,
Margaret, the color has lasted—all through
the hard, cold winter of our changes.
Look how the color has lasted.

FROM THE OUTSIDE NOW

FROM THE OUTSIDE NOW

Remembered from the outside now:
congregations, that slow
procession down the aisle,
pretension
to power. Remembered:
Amazing Grace, and *wretch like me.*

Free of that entanglement
except as the swimmer who has almost drowned
forever feels the pull of water
in her dreams, I remember
as all recovered addicts still remember
the sweet narcotic reassurance:

choir and bass voice of the preacher,
slow-motion Sunday mornings before
dinner from the oven
served to stacked-up plates by father
passed around the table to mother
at the other end. Remembered

like childhood.
Like an old, familiar grief.
Like belief.

SWEET POTATO PIE

for Evelyn May

We were young together.
In a missionary school, cross
-legged, we sat side by side

on a dormitory bed talking
about sex, sweet potato pie
and Jesus.

I am older now. My hair is grey.
Determined to lose weight, you
say *My face will be more wrinkled.*

After thirty-three years I am divorcing
Mother Church, and you take vows
of High Church confirmation.

We sit and talk about our lives,
our needs and disappointments.
Loving you,

I think the subjects haven't changed so much,
except there's nothing more I need to know
about sweet potato pie.

BOY: 1944

Born in a farmhouse in Wisconsin
to immigrant John Jacob Heinrich
and his wife, Amelia, born
to sisters Rosalind and Evangeline,
he plows fields.
He dreams under sumac,
the dusty green berries, oval
leaves changing to scarlet.

He watches the barn burn,
helps to build another.
He mends fences, tractors, gear
for workhorses, plows,
and does not learn to spell.
His sisters tease
that he will someday marry Audrey,
redhead loudmouth in the fifth grade
at Norway Grove. He hears
the children of Norwegians call
his sister *Mrs. Hitler.*
He calls himself *not immigrant,*
says he will be somebody,
says he will live alone.

BOY: 1983

I work all day today, trying
to capture you. I watch you
turn the tractor alone
at the end of the row, wait
as you come down the line, Wisconsin

dirt sticking to the sweat
on the bare skin of your back,
but your eye is on a fencepost
to keep the row behind you plumb.

How could I think you'd see me,
brown boy? That was so long ago,
and even then we were children in
different times.

Right before you disappear
I try to tell you
there are rituals, you know,
snow and the ending of snowing,
seasons when saying "yes"
is no longer necessary, when
things that are not always plumb
can stay that way,
when all the world's not summer any more
and fields plowed too many times
can lie fallow.

HENDERSON SETTLEMENT

Frakes, Kentucky, 1954

The rain begins again.
Hits tin roofs in fat splats
like thunder: Appalachia.
Thin whistle of a train.
Stinking Creek runs red
as rusty nails in the deep
crotch of the hollow.

We are summering from college;
missionaries, we think. For fun
we rock the rope bridge over Stinking Creek,
laugh at local preachers, how they thump
the Bible, how the men all hang around
outside the church, their spit
dark, thick with Red Dog.

We are too young, too ignorant,
we haven't learned to read
lessons carved in bone: flesh
and blood as mortal implication.
Even so, we can't find one thing funny
in the cough that rattles Fanny Jane.

She tells us farther along
the hollow, down the two-track road,
past the shack where Auntie Opal lives,
somebody worships snakes. Somebody,
she says, *has an operatin still
and ain't no Feds runnin pick-up trucks*

ever gonna catch im at it, neither.
We listen, we think maybe late some night
we might sneak out down the hollow,
get to touch a sacred snake, taste
corn liquor for ourselves.
It's dangerous, she says, and has to stop
for coughing. She holds a finger up,
shakes her head, signifying No.

And we obey. We stay inside
the Settlement until September.
Then cold coils down
Pine Mountain, grey fog hangs heavy
in the hollows, and it's time to go
back north to college.
Although we do not say it to each other,
the rope bridge isn't thrilling any more.

SATURDAY NIGHT

It's raining.
People in this church want us to go.
It's nothing personal, they say.

All day you worked on your sermon,
read it to me page after page,
then told me tonight you'll throw it away
and try to move in the Spirit.

I pray in bits and pieces, *Please, God . . .*
and *Why?*

Rain breaks against the swollen buds of leaves
on the other side of this dark pane
of window glass. I can't see
beyond it. My face
reflected, stares at me.
It isn't personal.

Before you go to sleep I touch you
as you lie naked to the waist.
Do you love me? you ask,
and do not open your eyes.

For a long time we are silent,
the palm of my hand moving
along the familiar muscles of your shoulder,
your face.
We have loved this people, this church,
this place. We are letting go.

Yes, yes, I love you, I answer
but my words seem
small in all of this
that isn't personal.

I AM MISSING YOU

here
the walls are unfamiliar.

I have been talking on this narrow bed
with old friends, hearing of the ends
of marriages, the end
of love.

I put my hand out now
and touch the wall.

I told you when I left
There's chicken in the freezer,
and you said
No one really understands Saint Paul.

Fog lay along the lake all day today
blurring twigs, branches, sky —
only the trunks of trees were clear.

Here
I am missing you
(the walls are unfamiliar)
trying to remember
if we said goodbye.

AT THE SEA OF GALILEE

We arrived at the Sea of Galilee
at night
a full moon
lay across the sea
lights along the Golon Heights
made necklaces of war
a crown of gunpoints
on the head of peace
soldiers
armed with death
hid from each other
the silent moon
moved over Galilee
deaf and blind
while Jesus walked
upon the waters of the mind.

MÁIRE, WHO FEEDS THE WILD CAT

Behind the convent a wild
cat is ill. She sleeps
in a fine mist of rain
on the warm hood
of a cooling automobile.
She's sick, poor thing,
you say. You say
she's too sick to run away.

And you are cloistered here
uneasy now in all the old
familiar habits, awkward
in the raw world, its own
severe conventions, language
of fashion, innuendos. Rules.

From the window of the guesthouse
I study the convent walls,
the remote third floor
where no one may go but
nuns of your particular order.
The wall is fortress high
and fortress thick. Inside,
the sisters smile, repeating
and repeating one another's names:
Rosario, Saint Ambrose, Immaculate.

Outside, where a mist of rain
has chilled the bone of this day,
a wild cat watches,
too sick to run away.

for Máire O'Donohoe

SARAH LAUGHED

Let me tell you about Sarah. She was no fool. Not even angels pulled sheep skin over her eyes. She knew a thing for what it was. Old Abraham had humped on her for all those years of her rich flow, and nothing had come of it to Sarah, except blood and disappointment.

Abraham didn't do so bad. Sarah gave him Hagar, and Hagar gave him a son. Hagar sat on Sarah's lap and let the baby drop between the thighs of Sarah. That was supposed to make everything all right. But Sarah couldn't seem to fool herself. She tried everything the rules and regulations would allow. And then quit trying. She sent Hagar and the bawling boy out into the wilderness. Cut them off. Let them go. As far as she could know, they would die.

So when some wandering fool came reassuring Abraham that sure enough, after all these years of blood between her knees, and some other woman's baby falling through her thighs, and nothing, nothing ever quite enough to get the promise God and Abraham seemed to have in mind; when someone making out to be an angel said Sarah, drying like a pomegranate around the useless seeds, would open her legs, open her life, and break like a young tree into blossom, Sarah laughed. She stood behind the tent flap listening to the men talk about what would come into her, and out of her, and Sarah laughed.

Well, it all happened the way the angel said, I guess. One more time, father Abraham lay his length along the hills and valleys of his wife, rained his semen into her dark cave, and this time, by god, he made himself a son.

And Sarah, we are led into supposing, was just as happy about the promise given unto Abraham as he was. That was in the days before he had to take the boy up on the mountain and lay him on the altar. No one says what Sarah was doing behind the tent flap in that scene. Maybe she had it figured out ahead of time and took a ram up the slope before her husband and her son began the climb.

For whatever reason, a ram did manage to get himself caught by the horns in a patch of bramble, just in the nick of time to save Isaac from the sacrificial fire, and incidentally, to save the promise given unto Abraham. The Bible gives the credit to the Lord. Maybe so.

Anyway, it's Sarah we remember, hiding there behind the flap laughing at the absurdity of angels. She was no angel. Hagar and Ishmael had a devil of a time out there in the desert, and for no better reason than Sarah, not believing someone else's promise any more.

LETTING GO

As a beggar, resting in the sun,
Peels off layers of her outer rags,
Astonished to discover that each one
Reveals another under it, her paper bags

Filling with the garments she had worn
When everything was harder, darker, colder;
As she feels the chill of being born
Again, wiser now, and older,

So I. Having shed the church in the belief
That one particular chill of letting go
Might be a kind of ultimate relief,
(A flat sun of contradiction, saying *No*

To winter, to the ice around the heart,)
Under vestments I am finding near the skin
Ragged garments where all distinctions start.
I blunder toward the person I had been

Before costuming for the beggar's part
And trying out in someone else's show.
Living now is nakedness of heart;
Dying — just another letting go.

PERSONAL ADDRESS

To you only I speak,
although you are forever
changing names, places
of residence, appearance,
affect. Reputation.

When I was a child
you hovered in the rafters
of the tabernacle, above
the visiting evangelist's head.
My mother said I should repent,
and so I did. Of what,
I have forgotten. I was
five years old. I do remember
how the tree, under which she knelt
and prayed with me for my salvation,
bore a single peach that year:
the hard, green bud of it. How
all the summer long I watched it grow.

There was something that I asked of you
in that worn-out orchard.
Although I don't remember what it was
I asked, I do know
I took the peach for answer.

DEAR LOVER, DEAR GOD,

How far shall I go to meet you?
Will you turn at the moment
where that sheer cliff meets the air,
the air, there, where only that small bird
belongs to both — cliff and air —
will you turn, will you speak my name,
and will that syllable mean welcome?
Will the silence that surrounds my name
mean home?

TRUTH ENOUGH

TRUTH ENOUGH

How much hair do I have? you ask,
sitting straight upon the kitchen stool.
I circle you, cut the fine filigree
silver over your ear.

I tell you the truth: Enough.
There is an echo at the edges of the word
which is the lie: Why, love, you still
have lots and lots of hair!

I have always told you the truth.
Even when you didn't want to know it,
not all of it, I mean, and if I had my life
to live again from the beginning, all
those choices, I might pick kindness
more, let truth alone to ripen on the tree.

But it is your hair I am cutting
on this ordinary afternoon,
and I am making love,
the circle of white on the kitchen floor
an aura. How black, how thick your hair
was! How in the steamy kitchen,
four children underfoot, grapes picked
for jelly tumbled in the colander, fruit jars
hot, baked bread sliced to steaming slabs
and everywhere outside the crimson leaves
falling — there in that confusion,
did I cut your hair?

Today the house is silent. Leaves fall,

but they do not seem to clatter
red against the gold the way they used to do.

Our children watch us delicately from portraits
on the wall. After all,
you say, how much hair do I have?

Enough, I say. I don't want to talk.
There is an aura on the kitchen floor,
and I am making love.

ORNAMENT

In a blue Christmas ornament
the family is reflected
tiny and upside down:
the older sister,
her perpetual performance;
the younger sister,
applauding; the brother,
standing sideways between them.
This ritual is frozen, fragile
as the single mind that remembers.

Outside, the streets are faithful.
They keep their accustomed crossings.

POND IN THE RIVER

*From an old map of rivers
in Maine*

Pond in the river . . . my son
says the name as if it were music.
The Alagash, Amherst Mill River,
the Amazon he says he will travel
with Warren, or Dave, or his sisters.

I pack his things into the attic:
Raggedy Andy,
the train set he gave to his sister.

He's taking his Narnia Series, so
I pray to the great Lion, Aslan,
to stand guard in his room at the college
against dragons and unicorn dangers.
I pray every music of morning
to bring his canoe through white water
and every evening a harbor.

I pray him a pond in the river.

LETTER TO A SON IN COLLEGE

I am sending you some money.

What I am not telling you
in this bright commercial card
is that I dreamed last night
your dying, dreamed
you drowning at an edge
of ocean between your green canoe
and a wooden coffin, dreamed
a man standing beside me on the shore,
saying *I don't see why it happened;
I told him to put the canoe in the coffin.*

I told your father, *We have lost
Paul.* I told your sisters.
Then I was alone with my grieving,
trying to understand why it was required
of you to put the canoe in the coffin
when I could see how you were trying,
and how with all those waves around you
it could not be done.

I know, my son, it is my ocean,
my canoe and my coffin
I am dreaming of. But just in case,
I'm sending you some money.
Don't let anyone tell you what to do
with your canoe.

SHAPE AND LINE. TOMORROW

My son, his throat bare
above a tattered T-shirt,
peels asbestos siding
from this old frame house
and stands back at the road edge,
the dust of fifty-year-old paint
on his young skin.

He breathes. The house breathes.

He does not smile. His eyes
are measuring effect, he is
da Vinci, inventing
shape and line. Tomorrow
he will spread out color charts.
He says, *It doesn't matter.
Any color you and Dad want is fine.
This is not my house.*
He is grown up now. In September
he will move away.

Summer passes, and he becomes
an intimate of every wasp
coming out from under
every eave. He learns
the secrets of the drainpipes,
the inside curve of every arch
of the porch's gingerbread.

He swears, he sings
*Ain't misbehavin', savin'
all my love for you!* He yells

at his kid sister for leaving
his new record on the stereo.
He'll be damned if he'll go
to the store for another can of paint.
He went to school with the Shumway kids
and what will they think
at Shumway's Paint and Wallpaper?
Good painters, he says, *don't get it
on their clothes and eyes and hair.*
But he goes. And at the end
of August, I hear him on the phone
saying to a friend, long distance,
I'm painting my house this summer.
Yeah, he says in answer to a question.
My own house.

OVERNIGHT

for Nina

The day your son calls you on the telephone
and is no more your boy, you know
he is someone else's man.
Hi, Mom! he calls across a chasm.
You guess the joy that carved it,
and you cry, *Hello!*

She will be the bridge, now,
between you and your son.
Overnight he has become shy with you.
Now that he knows her secret
he has guessed your own, guessed
the journeys that his father made
to fetch a son from darkness
on the other side of utter letting go.

Hello, you say, and suddenly remember
how in the fourth grade he brought a pigeon home.
How, as if it were an ordinary coming home,
he opened the front door, walked in and called,
Hi, Mom! How his eyes were pleading,
with love, like pinions, feathering the air.

TOMITA: PICTURES

> ... *the roll of thunder has been proved to be*
> *the sound caused by an electric phenomenon—*
> *that is, it is an electronic sound.*
> —Isao Tomita, notes on the record jacket,
> *Tomita: Pictures at an Exhibition*

This music my daughter plays
is in a foreign tongue.
I used to lean into a well
when I was a child, call
my own name into that dark
to make a distant music;
ninety feet down to water, listen
to my name come back from a place
that even in daylight
perfectly reflected stars.

My daughter says, *Listen!*
there's no human voice in this music.
Mom, isn't that amazing?

I hear voices. I answer,*Yes,*
amazing. I am ashamed
to tell her that something
in the music makes me dizzy, something
makes me almost feel afraid.

And yet, until this moment
I had forgotten how my own name sounded
coming back from water
ninety feet down, dark,
and even in the daytime,
full of stars.

TO A HIGH SCHOOL SENIOR

Don't go. Don't stay.
Daughter. Morning after afternoon
the last year slips away.

Singing all the old songs, you will go
(ambivalence of moon, certainty of sun)
we know

only half of what we are.
The earth is earth to us, star
perhaps

if apprehended far enough away.
Daughter — don't go.
Don't stay.

GRASSES LIKE A CURTAIN

At the edge of the supermarket lot
where asphalt gives up its flat dominion
there has grown up a field of grasses
higher than our heads.

I am on my way to buy a chicken;
there will be guests for dinner,
I have things to do. But you
are seventeen, six weeks from going off
to college, and besides, yesterday
it rained, a vast extravagance of storm
as if the Midwest you have chosen
sent its weather here, to charge you
with a wild, electric promise:
Your life will be your own.

The air is crystalline above the cars,
above the supermarket sign, above
the grasses. *Oh, look!* you cry.
Come on! You are heading for the field.

I stop just where the lip of asphalt
lays its gum against the world.
You open the grasses like a curtain
made of green glass hanging beads
and walk on in. A wind
moves in the field. The field sighs.

You stand, heads of grasses swaying
all around your hair. Then turn, laughing,
back to me. Where I am,
a caterpillar makes its careful way

up a stalk of grass. You bend to it,
hold a finger in its path, say
*You're on the very outside blade of grass,
you silly thing!* and carry it far back
into its forest of green stems.
You set the caterpillar free.

Then you return, for six more weeks, to me.

AFTER ALL, THE LEAVES

Have the leaves already turned?
you ask, pleading, on the telephone.
Today a bird smashed against the windowpane
and left a smear of tiny feathers on the glass.
I went out imagining that I would bring it in,
but the bird was gone.

Last October was your first away at college.
I didn't pay attention to the colors;
they were unbearable, so bright,
so without reason for their celebration.
Now I have grown a bit accustomed to your room
bare of clutter, the pictures
hung on its blue walls as orderly
as that little shoe box diarama
you carried under your left arm to second grade.

Today, after you called,
I walked along the sidewalk of our street
under the old maple trees. I thought
about how fast the colors change.
Already they are pretty far along
into their turning, some branches scarlet,
burnt against the blue October sky.
I want to say you'd better hurry home.
But then there was that bird.
If it had needed any help at all,
it would have needed help to fly away.
And it didn't.

CHILD

*Mom, I dreamed I had another
brother, younger than Paul.
He was gentle, and very fair.*

I didn't want that baby,
didn't even ask
was it a girl? A boy?

There was blood
before the time for blood
and I was glad.

The pale remembrance
of a child I did not see
nor name, nor bless,

even after all these years
remains a spiritual parenthesis
in the litany of names.

FIRST BORN

> *You may be tempted mid-retreat*
> *to levity.*
> — Sister Rita Anne

This retreat is silent.
Silently, my daughter, I watch you run.
From this high porch I watch you
trace the line where fields and forest meet.
You stop, a small, skin-colored dot
beside a distant pond.

When you return, you whisper:
The pond belongs to algae.
You couldn't swim. *The bank*
belongs to dragonflies.
Your brown skin, brown hair and eyes,
your clown face knows perfectly
—has practiced — how to make me laugh.
Across the table from each other,
we control temptation,
trembling with levity
all through the solemn meal.
Sister Rita is not the slightest bit
amused.

I am supposed to pray for peace,
for this world's suffering population,
for all things heavy and hard.
I can't. I am filled with hoping
you will someday have a daughter
who will run away

beyond the point where you can clearly see,
and then run back to you, whispering
news of blueblack algae
and pulse of dragonflies.
May she tempt you
beyond all possible control
to levity.

THE FACE OF THE OTHER

THE FACE OF THE OTHER

1.
The face of the other is not a mirror,
is perhaps a stream of running water
with occasional reflecting pools, is
perhaps a rain barrel, collecting
on its dark surface
fragments of sky, pieces
of the face that is bending above it.
But the face of the other is not turned
to this world, or to me,
as a mirror.

2.
In her eye, the right eye, behind the black
hole of her pupil, there is a scar
on the retina of my daughter's eye. The eye
that seems to see you
does not. Refuses the image,
catches some tangent irrelevance
to your left, but does not,
cannot admit you. Slowly,
as you are talking with her, you find
yourself meeting her through her left eye.
Without knowing why,
you go toward the opening that will
receive you, caress you,
take you in.

3.
Nowhere on this planet is there sanctuary.
It is a myth that we have played with,
dragging it like a favorite blanket

down the stairs from the nursery. Nowhere
is there sanctuary. And one half of all the eyes
to which we reveal ourselves cannot see us.

When the roar of the furnace stops
in the center of the night
and snow outside makes a silence
like that which we imagine might have been
before the world began,
which is to say before these particular ears
first heard the heartbeat of the furnace
just beyond the skin wall of the womb —
and when the absence of electric light,
and lost stars beyond collapsing snow
make a darkness like that which we imagine
might have been before the world began,
which is to say before these particular eyes
first opened in the water of the womb
to a dim filter of pink light —
when in the center of the night
we are awake in that silence, in that dark,
we may wonder at the insomnia of God,
wonder whether the face of God is a mirror,
whether the eyes of God take us in,
give us sanctuary,
or whether God, too, holds us in tension,
one eye caressing, the other closed,
mysterious, looking inward,
belonging only to God.

GOING HOME THE LONGEST WAY AROUND,

we tell stories, build
from fragments of our lives
maps to guide us to each other.
We make collages of the way
it might have been
had it been as we remembered,
as we think perhaps it was,
tallying in our middle age
diminishing returns.

Last night the lake was still;
all along the shoreline
bright pencil marks of light, and
children in the dark canoe pleading
Tell us scary stories.
Fingers trailing in the water,
I said someone I loved who died
told me in a dream
to not be lonely, told me
not to ever be afraid.

And they were silent, the children,
listening to the water
lick the sides of the canoe.

It's what we love the most
can make us most afraid, can make us
for the first time understand
how we are rocking in a dark boat on the water,
taking the long way home.

for Sharleen Kapp

WHITE RIVER JUNCTION

Fields white
with Queen Anne's Lace.
You want to talk of marriage.
Your voice trembles on the telephone:
Mother, shall I live with him?

I think of fear
and love. You were the child
we went to bed for.
Now I am driving north
to you. I say
I have no easy answers.

Mountains rise on either side.
New tassels on the summer corn
are grey-green and gold. Old
glacial drumlins, tumbled stone,
backbone of these mountains.
I was a child in mountain country.

It is change I am thinking of.

Here I cross a river. This high
bridge. How could I reach you
but in this arching up and out?

When I was small I played
along the edges of the Merrimac.
There were caves along that river.
Searching through the rocks
for fossils and for arrowheads,
I found stalactite fragments and

I thought of rivers flowing
underground. What does it mean
to love, to marry, and is purity
of heart destroyed by our occasions?

Neither you nor I are children
any more. The signs are clear:
White River Junction
must be somewhere straight ahead.

I have wondered sometimes whether
another way
would have been more smooth.
There are places where the road
divides. The eye
always sees more than the hand
can hold. These old mountains,
their stones, their moss,
are held in place by roots
of evergreen. And Queen Anne's
Lace. My wedding gown.
I would have to hold my breath
to fit it now.

Fields are white with lace, froth
like foam floating on a sea of grass.
Those white circles
pinwheels, Ferris wheels,
cartwheels within a wheel.
I have no answers.

Never knowing names of grasses,
I have loved the arching
of their bending, the spike,
the cut, clean edges of their blades.
I want to show you how their heads
grow in complexity

until they drop and shatter,
letting the form of what they had become
transform under snow.

Perhaps the error in the primal garden
was not so much the tasting
of sweet, forbidden fruit
as it was the naming of the beasts,
reducing them to definition,
naming that, which named,
we could not meet:
wilderness,
bouquets of wild things,
Daughter.

A BLESSING

Today I boiled fifty pounds of potatoes after I washed
Connecticut valley, river valley, soil from their smooth skins.
My daughter will be married on Sunday. We will fill a pew
again, her sisters, her brother her father and I, and sing the
old hymn, — *Joyful, Joyful We Adore Thee* — as we sang at
our own wedding, at each child's baptism, at our first
daughter's wedding, at a best friend's funeral. *Joyful, joyful,
we adore Thee, God of glory, Lord of love* . . . and Peter
will speak from the front of the sanctuary as he did on every
Sabbath for twenty five years, and I am washing river
bottom soil from the smooth skin of these potatoes and the
sun on this October day is saffron on the leaves of birch
trees, scarlet on the maples, and this soil is falling, falling
through my fingers, see how fine and rich it is and how do
you bless the marriage of a daughter if you are a woman and
you know the way by heart that has been your own way but
you know you do not know anything more? How? How
do you bless her, other than this, to lay your hand on the
satin dress and say *yes, this seam is all right now, this lace
will do,* — and make the dozens of fancy cookies wearing
the apron you wore to help her make paper mache, model
clay, learn to cook — how do you bless her other than this,
to lay down your day, your morning, your afternoon, your
life, saying *look how fine, how rich is this river bottom soil
— how it is so smooth beneath my fingers* — *look what the
earth has made hidden in the dark soil: these potatoes. Take
them to the back porch to cool. Tomorrow we will make
potato salad for the wedding feast. Go now, quickly, while
I clean the sweet soil from the sink.*

BRAIDED RUG

The rug is braided and the braid
is the hair of a woman and the air
is full of birds that are not singing
and I am very tired. What am I
going to do if this is not the clue
to something   and here it is
almost October and no crocuses
are planted on the lawn and here
       it is
  half way through my life
     and
the rug is braided and the braid
is a path and the crimson
is the blood of a boy
dying by himself in a swamp
in a war that he does not believe in,
does not understand, and the blue
is his father's eyes trying to believe,
trying to understand, and the white
is the blank evidence of blue
and crimson, and the stitches
that hold the braid coming around this time
to the braid that came around last time,
     the stitches
  are the mother. She holds
    it all together.
But maybe if she didn't, maybe
the crimson would flow off to a flower
in the corner of a pasture under gooseberry
bushes and blue
would maybe go back into sky and white

would not be absence any more
but presence
of snow cut to puzzle pieces by stalks
of wild iris
in the center of the circle
where the first braid turns back on itself,
like an iris in the eye of God.

TROUBLE

The day comes on disguised as headache.
The body is a tremor of the day.
There is no known way to escape
the town named trouble.
Say magic, say religion,
say every song you can remember,
nothing will open the gate.
Sorrow sits outside the window.
It's eyes are the eyes of a pigeon;
it dirties the place where it stands.
You wait. The day comes down.
You touch your fingers to your temples.
Headache, you say. The pigeon
lifts one foot, tucks it under its feathers.
A film comes slowly down over its eyes.

LUCIA THERESA: NICARAGUA, 1985

Lucia Theresa is raped by eight solders,
first with their cocks,
then with the barrels of rifles.

Her young sons watch from the corner.

The soldiers explain:
they are punishing Lucia Theresa
for the escape of her little daughter.
The child ran naked into the street
and hid in the home of a neighbor.

I am writing about my daughters.
I say the name: *Lucia Theresa.*

Her name is a name for women:
faces of women refugees on the evening news,
bodies of women sleeping on the floor
of the train station in New York City,
women raped, disappeared, dismembered,
women telling their little girls never to walk alone
on any street in any town at night,
women denied jobs at the tops of corporations,
women nameless in housing projects
all across this land where Ronald Reagan
told the bitter lie: there is no hunger here.

So I name her name
because I do not know what else to do:
Lucia Theresa.

WILD WOLVES HOWLING

I play a tape of wild wolves howling
in my kitchen on a winter afternoon
and turn to find the cat transfixed
in the pantry, her eyes propped wide
with terror, unable to decide whether
there are wolves along the counter,
in the refrigerator, or coming in the door.

Poor puss. I tell her there are no wolves
left in the hill towns any more,
but she is not consoled. She knows
something I don't know, with teeth,
that has dominion in our neighborhood,
takes bites out of her fur at night,
and leaves her bloody.

Death still lives in the tall pine tree
beside our house, and under the garden shed,
and in the neighbor's patch of oriental bamboo.
Death floats some nights disguised
as moon, that fat clown face growing
each night thinner. I hear the name
of another young man gone to AIDS

and play the sound of wild wolves howling,
as if for a little while to keep at bay
the silent dark that nibbles at the moon.

DON'T LOOK AT THE MOON

You talk to your daughter
about her divorce. She says
I have to leave this place;
there are memories everywhere.

You listen.
You can hear the green plant growing
in the sunlight in her window.
At night she tells you
don't look at the moon.
It's too beautiful, riding
the black oak branches.

She is packing her bags to go.
All that you know is not enough.

DEATH AS HOUSEPLANT

Death stands in the corner
opposite the metal fruitcake tin
where we keep the aspirin
and the Tylenol.

Until today, I mistook him
for a houseplant,
leaning toward the window,
hungering for light
in this New England winter.

Becky was crying on the telephone:
*Mama, I'm so sick,
I've never been so sick!
It's the Taiwan flu — I've got
black spots on my tongue —
Oh, Mama —*

and my mind divided, one half
thinking, Antibiotics. Doctors.
But the other half seemed to be not me,
seemed to be a woman a hundred years ago
looking at black spots
on her daughter's tongue,
hearing: *Mama. Mama.*

While I was saying, *Honey, go to bed—
let someone else care for your baby,
—do you want me to come . . .*

death turned his face toward me
and dropped a leaf,
its veins still green and fragrant
on the kitchen floor.

BRIDGE

On the other side of the continent
my last child is twenty-one.
I have been given a room
with a view of the Golden Gate —
water and sky and long line
of lighted hills: San Francisco
and Marin and in between
the bridge.
I myself am a city set on a hill.
My children can't forget me
even if they try. They move away.
I recite their names:
Rebecca. Laurel. Bethany. Paul.
Distant cities;
separate civilizations.
From this room I can see the lights
of San Francisco coming on. And now
the Bay Bridge is a string of amber lights.
But I am waiting for the bridge lights
on the Golden Gate. I wait and wait.
They don't come on. Instead,
the whole bridge slowly disappears into dark.
Years ago, carrying my first baby in my belly
up and down this hill, didn't I see the bridge
at night light up like a visitation?
I recite the names of cities I have learned by heart:
San Francisco. And across the bay,
San Leandro. San Anselmo.
Dark has opened like a mouth.
The cities are connected by what I can remember;
they are held together by what I cannot see.

THIS FLIGHT

THIS FLIGHT

>   *Upon the birth of Sarah,
>   first grandchild.*

This flight, then, before the last.
Distance won,
centering in.

There were wild birds,
were there not? Feeding
from my fingers?

Or were they children?

This feathering is not down
bedding of ducks
wintering
on the pond, wings folded,
feeding from my fingers,
fingers of my children,
their bright faces bending
toward reflection.

This feathering is for flight.
I might think this
to be that other time,
mistake the wild bird for its image,
but for pinions.

I am still a long way from home
but turning now,
banking on air,
coming in.

WELCOMING ANGELS

Between the last war
and the next one,
waiting for the northbound train
that travels by the river,
I sit alone in the middle of the night
and welcome angels.
Welcome back old hymns, old songs,
all the music, the rhyme and rhythm,
welcome angels, archangels,
welcome early guesses
at the names of things,
welcome wings.

I have grown tired of disbelief.
What once was brave is boring.
Welcome back to my embrace stranger,
visitor beside the Jabbok.
Welcome wrestling until dawn,
until it is my hip thrown out of joint,
my pillow stone, my ladder
of antique assumptions.
Welcome what is not my own:
glory on the top rung, coming down.

THE TRAIL

O where can I go
where there will be no
sweet orange salamanders
almost underfoot, no
great bald eagles
circling above
Mount Toby tower,
no loved young climbers
ahead, higher on the hill
trail, no wild Sumac,
Sassafras, Solomon's
Seal bright red berries
draping the edge of the path?
This world is a feast;
I can feel it — and my life
is beginning to push me
away from the table.
There will come a day
when I will say, *Enough —
I am full of Glory.*

THINGS THE WIND DOES

Lifts a spatter of last night's raindrops
and flings them in my path.

Lifts a dozen leaves
and spins them for no good reason

Lifts the sound of my neighbor's voice.
(She is seventy five. I am fifty four.)

> *Let me see your new clothes.*
>
> *These aren't new clothes,*
> *I've just not worn them much.*
> *They're too hot.*
>
> *Too hot?*
>
> *Yeah, I'm having hot flashes.*
>
> *Primly tightening robe around her . . .*
> *Are you wearing underpants?*
>
> *Surprised . . . Yes.*
>
> *Take them off. Let the air*
> *blow up under your skirt.*

Lifts the sound of my youngest daughter's voice
singing, *Blessed are the last days of summer.*

for Eugenie Stacey

FIRST COUSIN

for Rozema Summers

Pelicans rest on rocks
off the shore near Monterey.
Awkward walking, they were
made to fly. We watch them
from the window of this restaurant
where we have ordered fish, and
let it cool. We talk
about our mother's lives, about
our brothers, our children.
Your face has grown so wrinkled;
my hair has turned so grey.
We know what we may say,
by heart what we must never say
to one another. Even so,
as the murmur of our voices
settles on the fish bones, floats
on dark circles of coffee,
it is our lives we offer to each other,
lay out on the table top, trying
to map the landscape spread
between us. We know
we will give up this awkward walk
some day. We name
common points of reference
so we will not lose our way.

MIDSUMMER

Midsummer. A child fussy with heat
screams in the cool bath, *No!*
Her mother holds her, speaks softly,
pours the cool water gently
on her hair, her back,
on the round, sweet curve of her belly.
Still she screams *No!*
She is afraid.

A curtain fills with the smell of rain.
Another child, afraid of the lightning,
hides under the bed. She is afraid
of the moan of the evening train,
afraid of snakes, afraid
of the bundle of sticks the KKK
left on the front porch as a warning.

It is midsummer.

I listen.
The first child is my granddaughter
on this muggy afternoon.
The other is my mother, eighty years ago.
Their voices meet here, collide and fall
into my fiftieth year.

Oak leaves, maple, sycamore,
all are now heavy with summer.
They rustle like voices of children.
They will dry, brown like old photographs
of children: granddaughter, mother,
daughter, father, son.

Here are some things to remember
in the evening, on a day in midsummer:
the child whose voice you hear
and the child whose voice you imagine.
The cat, belly down for cool
on the wide wooden boards of the floor;
lightning and thunder,
lightning bugs over the peonies
in the backyard when you were a child.
Your own silence, there at the screendoor,
rain
and the undersides of leaves
where you hoped lightning bugs hide
when the rain gets heavy.

THERE IS ANOTHER WAY

There is another way to enter an apple:
a worm's way.
The small, round door
closes behind her. The world
and all its necessities
ripen around her like a room.

In the sweet marrow of a bone,
the maggot does not remember
the wingspread
of the mother, the green
shine of her body, nor even
the last breath of the dying deer.

I, too, have forgotten
how I came here, breathing
this sweet wind, drinking rain,
encased by the limits
of what I can imagine
and by a husk of stars.